Teaching Little Fingers to Play
Easy Duets

10 Equal-Level Duets arranged by
Carolyn Miller

Cover Design by Nick Gressle

Book
ISBN 978-1-4234-8327-4

Book/CD
ISBN 978-1-4234-8238-1

EXCLUSIVELY DISTRIBUTED BY

HAL•LEONARD®
CORPORATION
7777 W. BLUEMOUND RD. P.O. BOX 13819 MILWAUKEE, WI 53213

Visit Hal Leonard Online at
www.halleonard.com

CONTENTS

Rock-a-Bye, Baby

SECONDO

TRACKS
1 – 3

Traditional
Arranged by Carolyn Miller

Play both hands one octave lower.

Like a soft Waltz

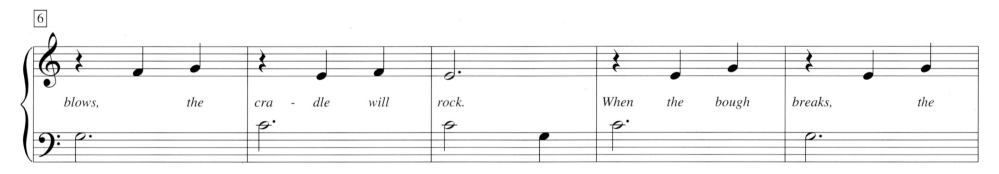

Rock-a-Bye, Baby

PRIMO

TRACKS
1 – 3

Play both hands one octave higher.

Traditional
Arranged by Carolyn Miller

Like a soft Waltz

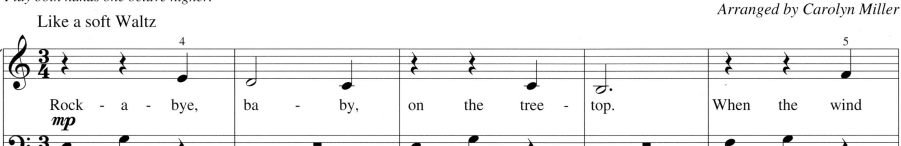

Rock - a - bye, ba - by, on the tree - top. When the wind

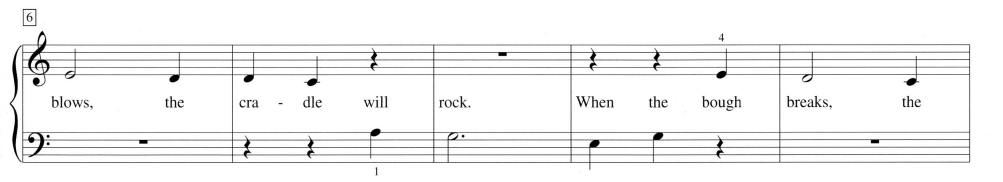

blows, the cra - dle will rock. When the bough breaks, the

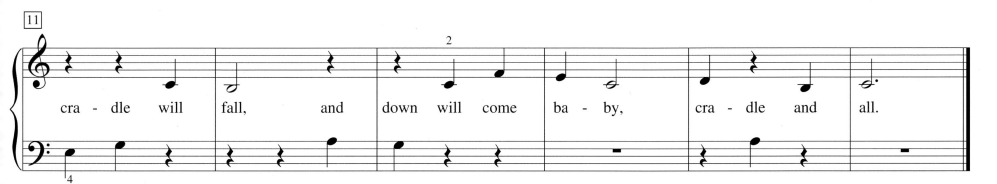

cra - dle will fall, and down will come ba - by, cra - dle and all.

London Bridge

SECONDO

TRACKS 4 – 6

Traditional
Arranged by Carolyn Miller

Play both hands as written.

With spirit

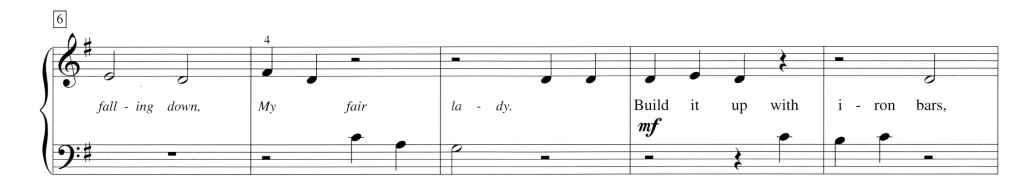

London Bridge

PRIMO

Traditional
Arranged by Carolyn Miller

TRACKS
4 – 6

Play both hands one octave higher.

With spirit

Lon - don Bridge is fall - ing down, fall - ing down, fall - ing down; Lon - don Bridge is

mf

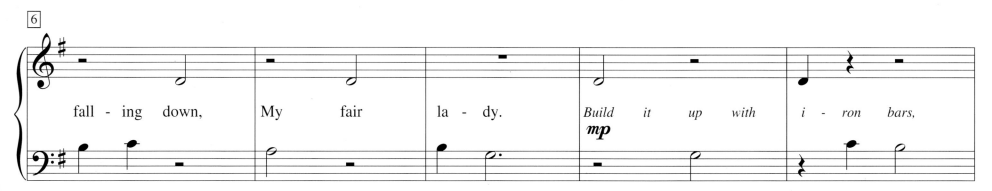

fall - ing down, My fair la - dy. *Build it up with i - ron bars,*

mp

i - ron bars, i - ron bars; Build it up with *i - ron bars,* My fair la - dy.

Alphabet Song

SECONDO

TRACKS 7 – 9

Play both hands one octave lower.

Traditional
Arranged by Carolyn Miller

Happily

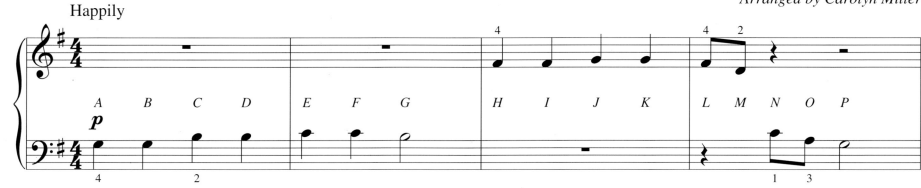

A B C D E F G H I J K L M N O P

Q R S T U and V, W (dou - ble U) X Y and Z.

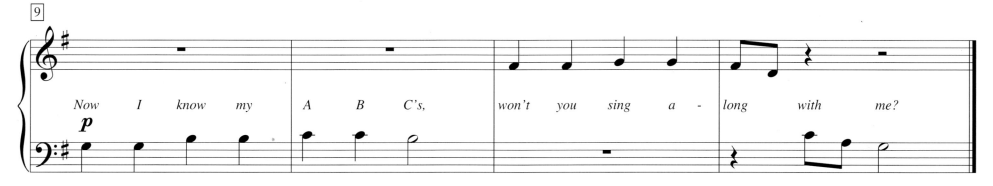

Now I know my A B C's, won't you sing a - long with me?

Alphabet Song

PRIMO

TRACKS
7 – 9

Play both hands one octave higher.

Traditional
Arranged by Carolyn Miller

Happily

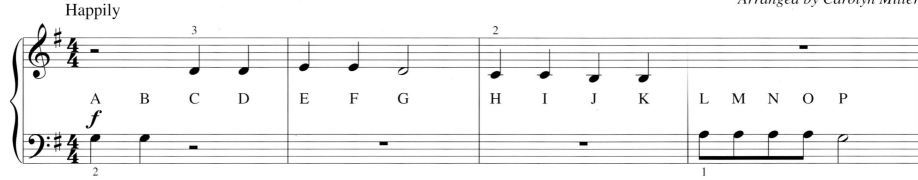

A B C D E F G H I J K L M N O P

Q R S T U and V, W X Y and Z.
(dou - ble U)

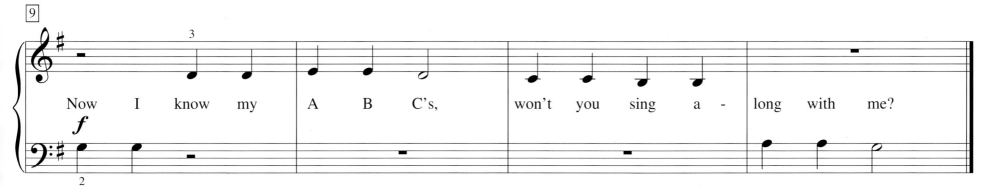

Now I know my A B C's, won't you sing a - long with me?

Mary Had a Little Lamb

SECONDO

TRACKS 10 – 12

Play both hands one octave lower.

Traditional
Arranged by Carolyn Miller

Mar - y had a lit - tle lamb, lit - tle lamb, lit - tle lamb. Mar - y had a

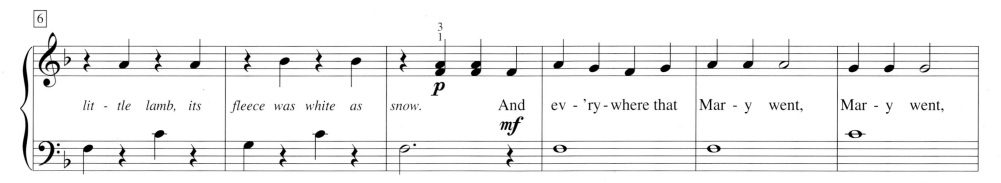

lit - tle lamb, its fleece was white as snow. And ev - 'ry-where that Mar - y went, Mar - y went,

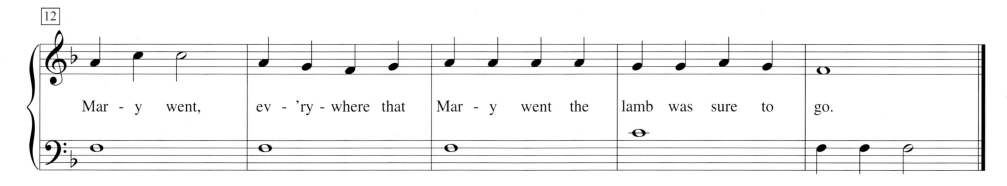

Mar - y went, ev - 'ry-where that Mar - y went the lamb was sure to go.

Mary Had a Little Lamb

PRIMO

Traditional
Arranged by Carolyn Miller

Play both hands one octave higher.

Sweetly

**TRACKS
10 – 12**

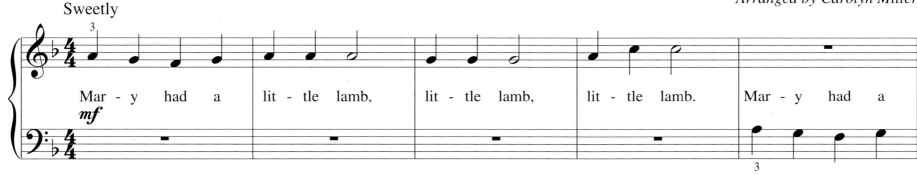

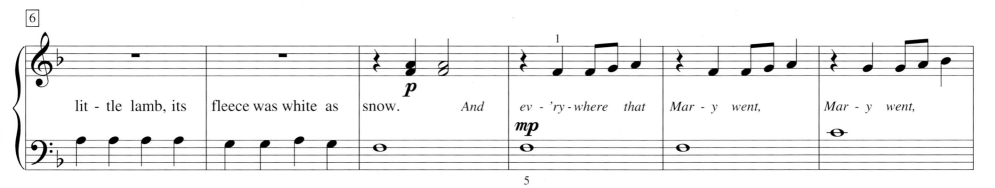

Old MacDonald

SECONDO

TRACKS
13 – 15

Play both hands one octave lower.

Traditional Children's Song
Arranged by Carolyn Miller

Lively, with an occasional 'quack' or 'moo'

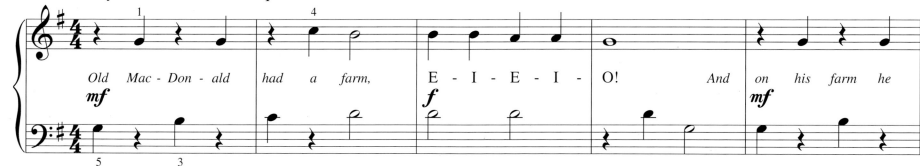

Old Mac-Don-ald   had   a   farm,   E - I - E - I - O!   And   on   his   farm   he

had   a   cow,   E - I - E - I - O!   With   a   moo-moo here,   moo-moo there,   here a moo, there a moo,

ev-'ry-where a moo - moo.   Old   Mac-Don-ald   had   a   farm,   E - I - E - I - O!

Old MacDonald

PRIMO

Traditional Children's Song
Arranged by Carolyn Miller

Play both hands one octave higher.

Lively, with an occasional 'quack' or 'moo'

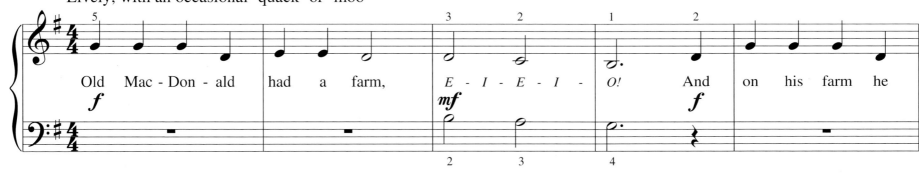

Old Mac-Don-ald had a farm, E - I - E - I - O! And on his farm he

had a cow, E - I - E - I - O! With a moo-moo here, *moo - moo there,* here a moo, *there a moo,*

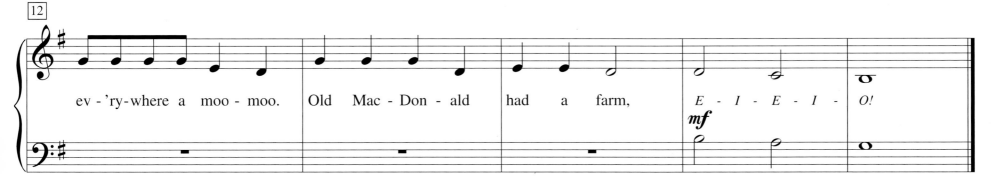

ev-'ry-where a moo - moo. Old Mac-Don-ald had a farm, E - I - E - I - O!

Eensy Weensy Spider

TRACKS
16 – 18

SECONDO

Traditional
Arranged by Carolyn Miller

Play both hands one octave lower.

Cautiously

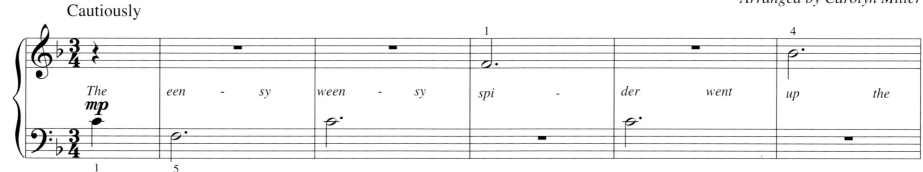

The een - sy ween - sy spi - der went up the

wa - ter - spout. Down came the

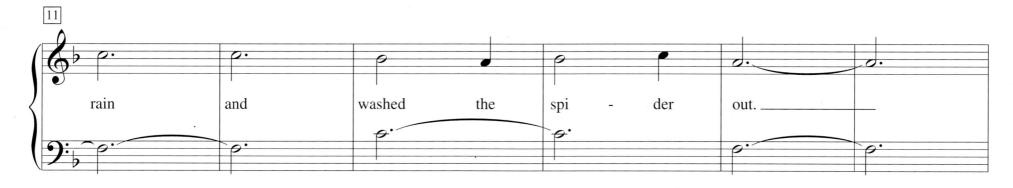

rain and washed the spi - der out. _____

Eensy Weensy Spider

PRIMO

TRACKS 16–18

Play both hands one octave higher.

Traditional
Arranged by Carolyn Miller

Cautiously

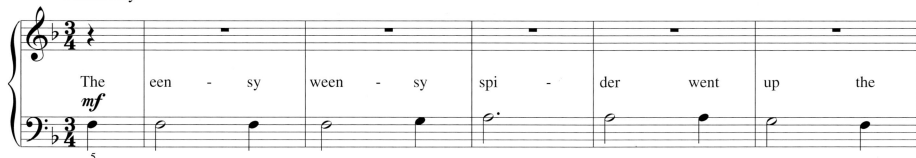

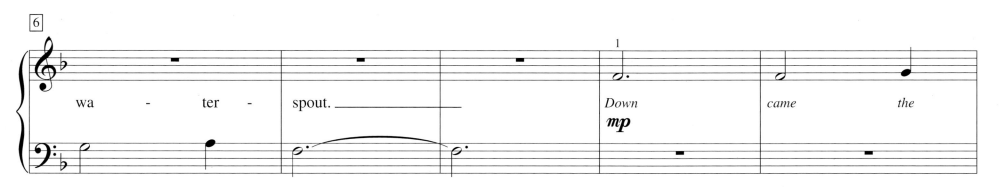

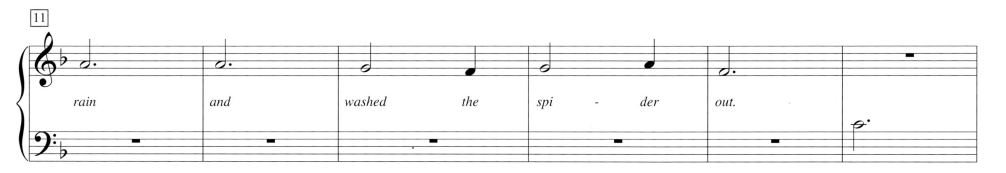

SECONDO

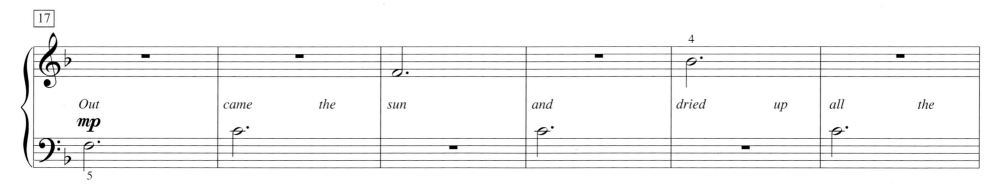

Out came the sun and dried up all the

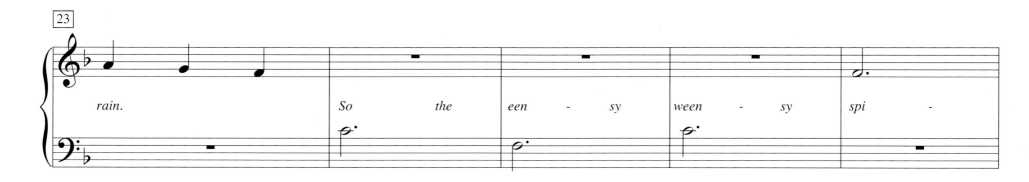

rain. So the een - sy ween - sy spi -

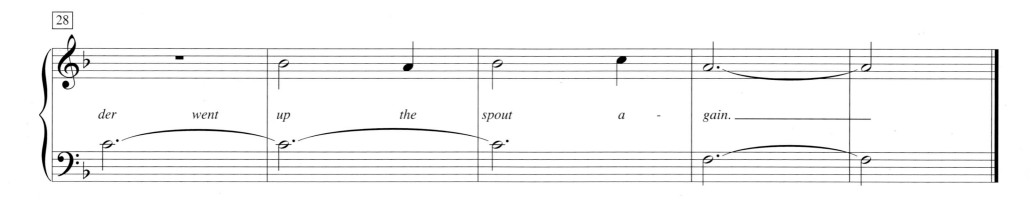

der went up the spout a - gain.

PRIMO

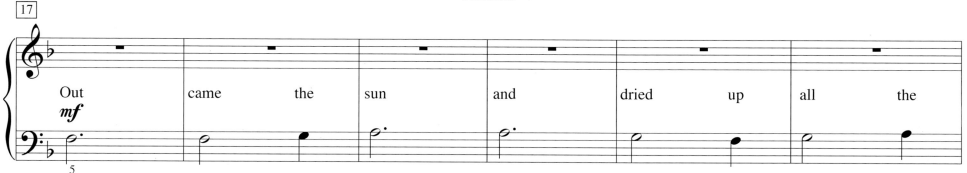

Out came the sun and dried up all the

rain. So the een - sy ween - sy spi -

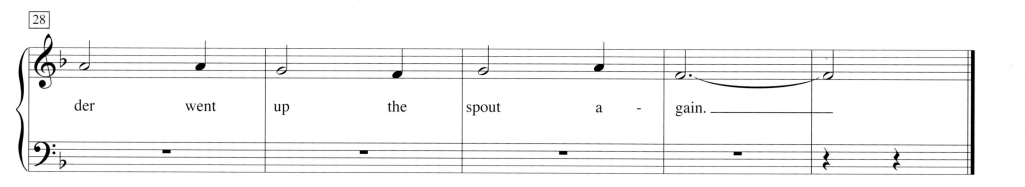

der went up the spout a - gain.

Row, Row, Row Your Boat

(A Musical Round)

SECONDO

TRACKS
19 – 21

Traditional
Arranged by Carolyn Miller

Play both hands one octave lower.

Steadily

Row, Row, Row Your Boat
(A Musical Round)

PRIMO

Traditional
Arranged by Carolyn Miller

TRACKS
19 – 21

Play both hands one octave higher.

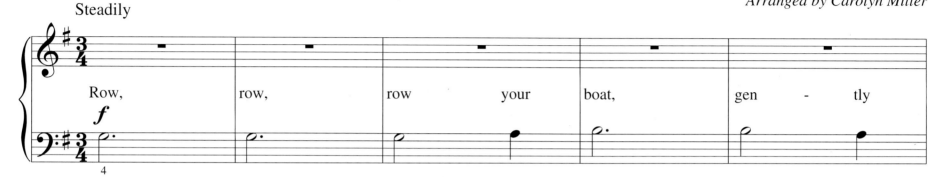

SECONDO

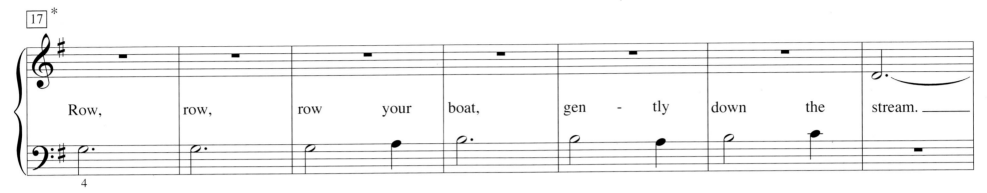

Row, row, row your boat, gen - tly down the stream. ____

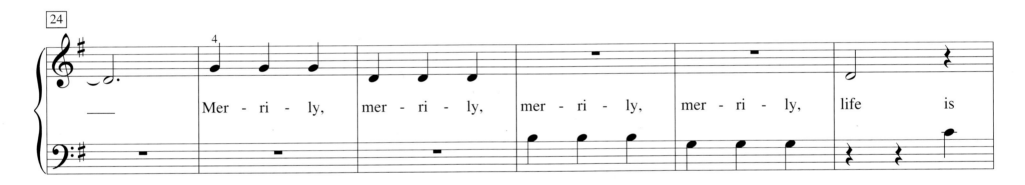

____ Mer - ri - ly, mer - ri - ly, mer - ri - ly, mer - ri - ly, life is

but a dream!

* The round for the Secondo begins at 17 .
  The round for the Primo begins at 21 .

PRIMO

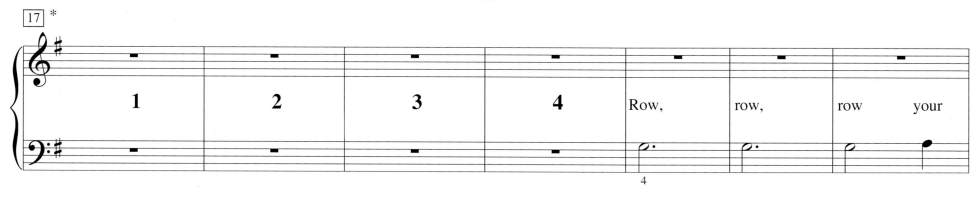

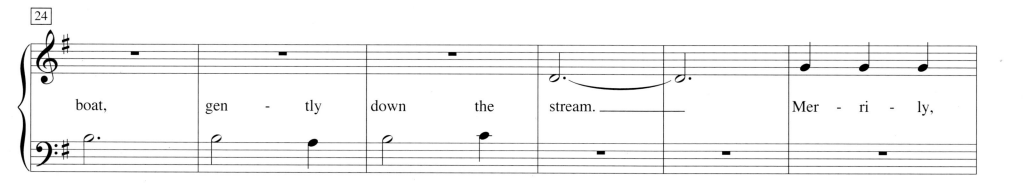

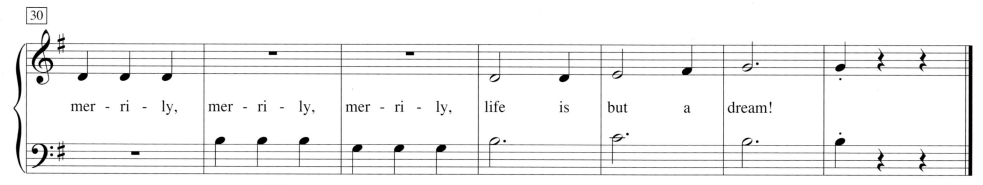

* The round for the Secondo begins at 17 .
   The round for the Primo begins at 21 .

Frère Jacques
(Are You Sleeping?)
SECONDO

TRACKS
22 – 24

Traditional
Arranged by Carolyn Miller

Play both hands one octave lower.

Quickly

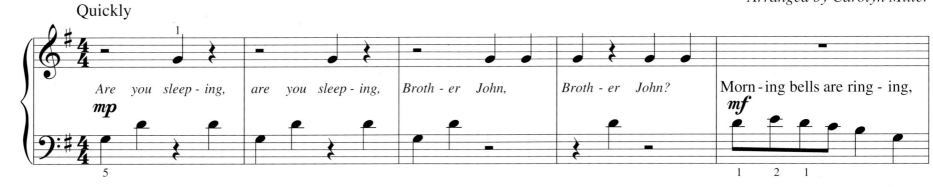

Are you sleep - ing, are you sleep - ing, Broth - er John, Broth - er John? Morn - ing bells are ring - ing,

morn - ing bells are ring - ing, *Ding ding dong,* *ding ding dong.* *Frè - re Jac - ques,* *Frè - re Jac - ques,* Dor - mez vous,

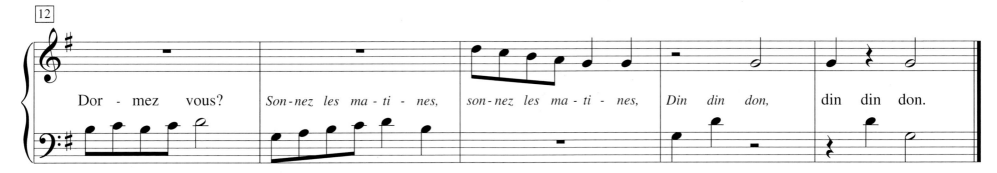

Dor - mez vous? *Son - nez les ma - ti - nes,* *son - nez les ma - ti - nes,* Din din don, din din don.

Frère Jacques

(Are You Sleeping?)

PRIMO

TRACKS
22 – 24

Play both hands one octave higher.

Traditional
Arranged by Carolyn Miller

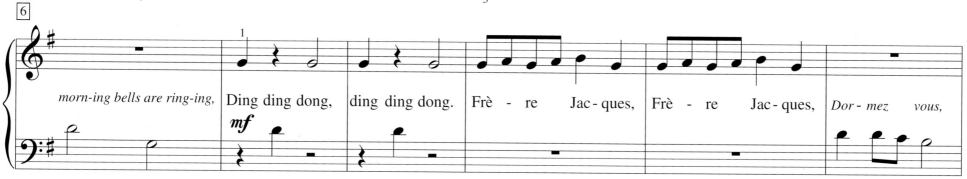

Animal Fair

SECONDO

American Folk Song
Arranged by Carolyn Miller

TRACKS 25 – 27

Play both hands one octave lower.

Moderately, mischievously

I went to the an-i-mal fair, _____ the birds and

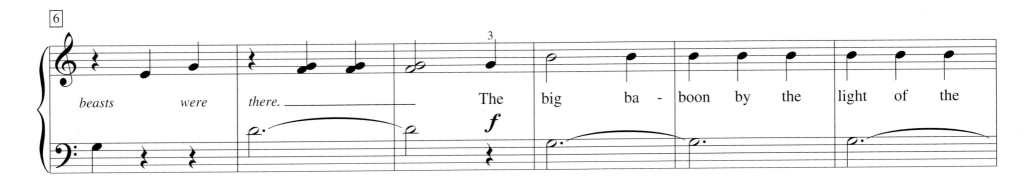

beasts were there. _____ The big ba-boon by the light of the

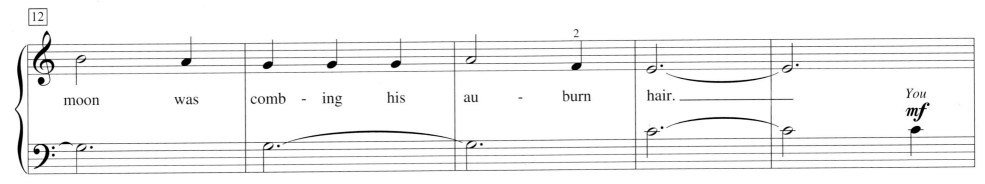

moon was comb-ing his au-burn hair. _____ You

Animal Fair

PRIMO

American Folk Song
Arranged by Carolyn Miller

TRACKS 25 – 27

Play both hands one octave higher.

Moderately, mischievously

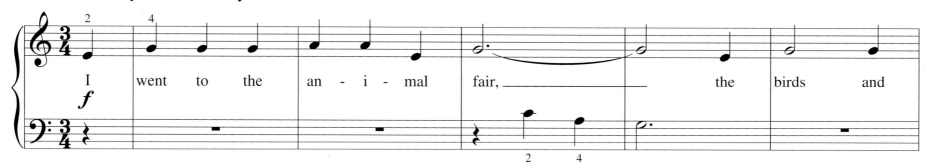

I went to the an - i - mal fair, _____ the birds and

beasts were there. _____ *The* big ba - boon by the light of the

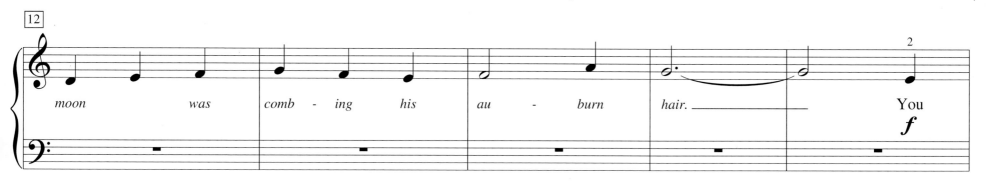

moon was comb - ing his au - burn hair. _____ You

should have seen the monk, _____ he sat on the el - e - phant's

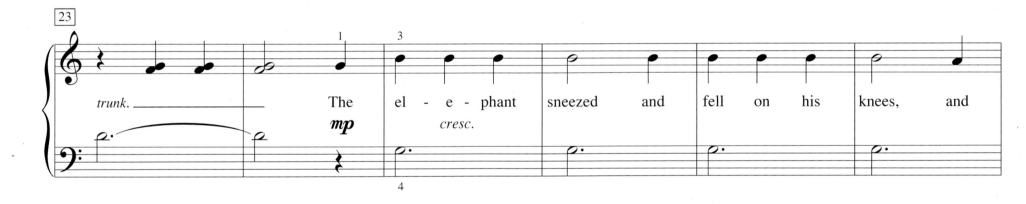

trunk. _____ The el - e - phant sneezed and fell on his knees, and

mp *cresc.*

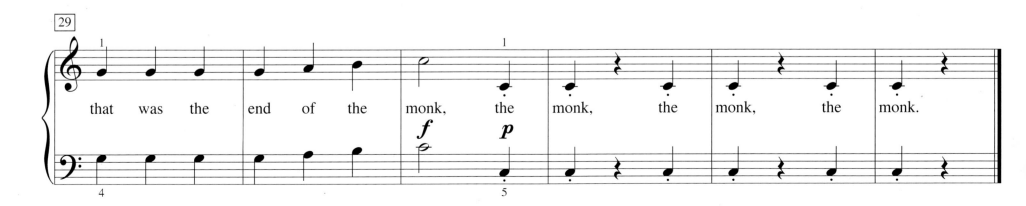

that was the end of the monk, the monk, the monk, the monk.

f *p*

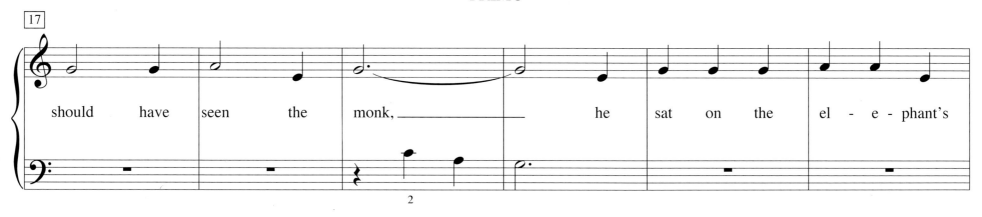

should have seen the monk, _____ he sat on the el - e - phant's

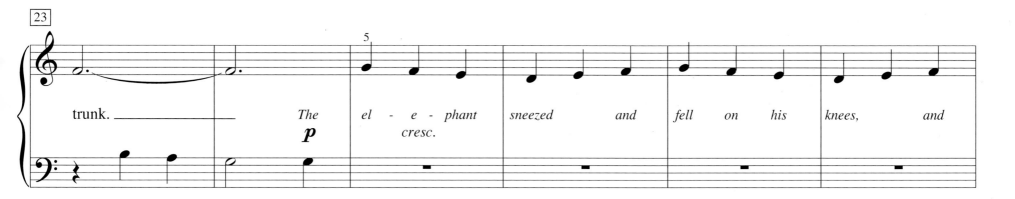

trunk. _____ The el - e - phant sneezed and fell on his knees, and

p   *cresc.*

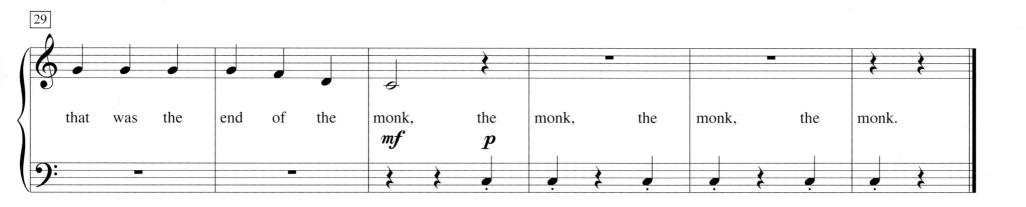

that was the end of the monk, the monk, the monk, the monk.

mf   *p*

For He's a Jolly Good Fellow

SECONDO

TRACKS
28 – 30

Traditional
Arranged by Carolyn Miller

Play both hands one octave lower.

With enthusiasm

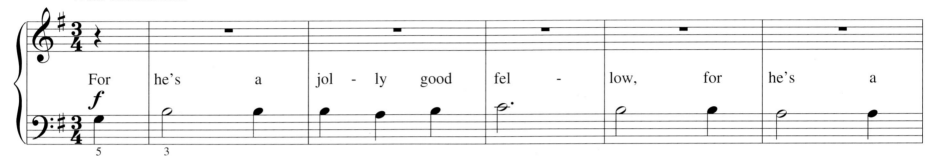

For he's a jol - ly good fel - low, for he's a

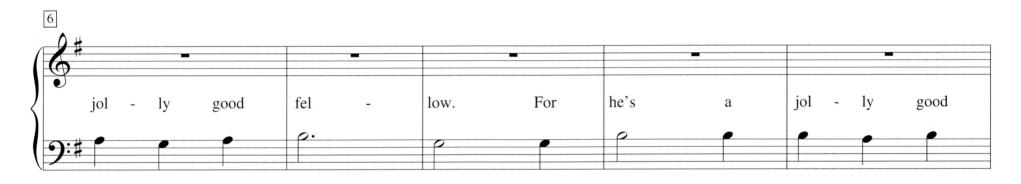

jol - ly good fel - low. For he's a jol - ly good

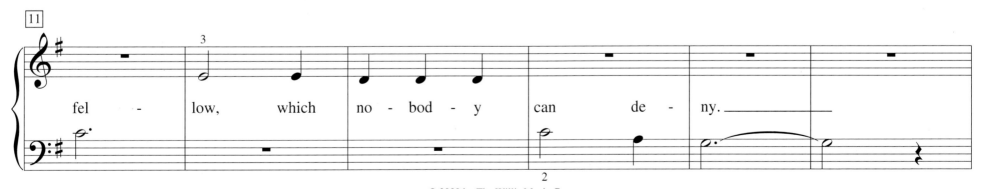

fel - low, which no - bod - y can de - ny. _____

2

For He's a Jolly Good Fellow

PRIMO

TRACKS
28 – 30

Play both hands one octave higher.

Traditional
Arranged by Carolyn Miller

With enthusiasm

Which

3

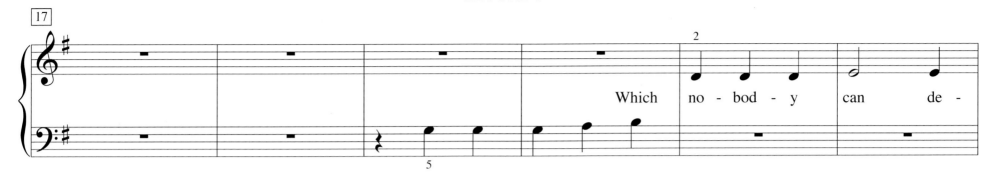

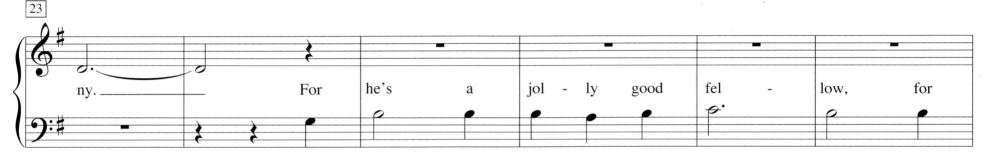

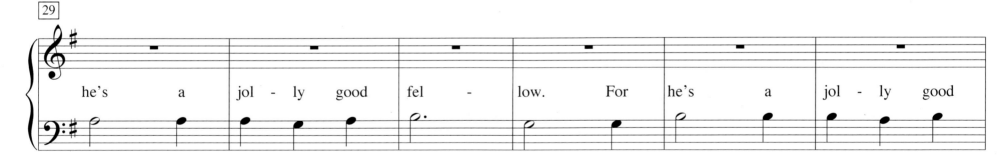

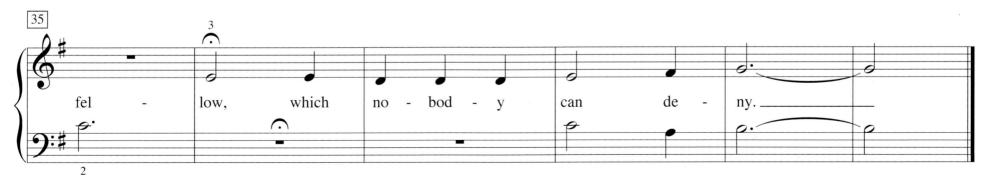

TEACHING LITTLE FINGERS TO PLAY

TEACHING LITTLE FINGERS TO PLAY

by John Thompson

A series for the early beginner combining rote and note approach. The melodies are written with careful thought and are kept as simple as possible, yet they are refreshingly delightful. All the music lies within the grasp of the child's small hands.

00412076 Book only $7.99
00406523 Book/Audio................................$10.99

TEACHING LITTLE FINGERS TO PLAY ENSEMBLE

by John Thompson

A book of intermediate-level accompaniments for use in the teacher's studio or at home. Two possible accompaniments are included for each *Teaching Little Fingers* piece: a Secondo or Primo part, as well as a second piano part for studios that have two pianos/keyboards.

00412228 Book only $6.99

DISNEY TUNES

arr. Glenda Austin

10 delightful Disney songs: The Bare Necessities • Can You Feel the Love Tonight • Candle on the Water • God Help the Outcasts • Kiss the Girl • Mickey Mouse March • The Siamese Cat Song • Winnie the Pooh • You'll Be in My Heart (Pop Version) • Zip-A-Dee-Doo-Dah.

00416748 Book only $9.99
00416749 Book/Audio................................$12.99

CHRISTMAS CAROLS

arr. Carolyn Miller

12 piano solos: Angels We Have Heard on High • Deck the Hall • The First Noel • Hark! The Herald Angels Sing • Jingle Bells • Jolly Old Saint Nicholas • Joy to the World! • O Come, All Ye Faithful • O Come Little Children • Silent Night • Up on the Housetop • We Three Kings of Orient Are.

00406391 Book only $7.99
00406722 Book/Audio....................................$10.99

CLASSICS

arr. Randall Hartsell

11 piano classics: Bridal Chorus (from *Lohengrin*) (Wagner) • Can-Can (from *Orpheus in the Underworld*) (Offenbach) • Country Gardens (English Folk Tune) • A Little Night Music (from *Eine kleine Nachtmusik*) (Mozart) • Lullaby (Brahms) • Ode to Joy (from Symphony No. 9) (Beethoven) • Symphony No. 5 (Second Movement) (Tchaikovsky) • and more.

00406550 Book only $7.99
00406736 Book/Audio...................................$10.99

HYMNS

arr. Mary K. Sallee

11 hymns: Amazing Grace • Faith of Our Fathers • For the Beauty of the Earth • Holy, Holy, Holy • Jesus Loves Me • Jesus Loves the Little Children • Joyful, Joyful, We Adore Thee • Kum Bah Yah • Praise Him, All Ye Little Children • We Are Climbing Jacob's Ladder • What a Friend We Have in Jesus.

00406413 Book only $7.99
00406731 Book/Audio....................................$10.99

TEACHING LITTLE FINGERS TO PLAY MORE

by Leigh Kaplan

Teaching Little Fingers to Play More is a fun-filled and colorfully illustrated follow-up book to *Teaching Little Fingers to Play*. This book strengthens skills learned while easing the transition into John Thompson's *Modern Course, Book One*.

00406137 Book only $6.99
00406527 Book/Audio...................................$10.99

MORE DISNEY TUNES

arr. Glenda Austin

9 songs, including: Circle of Life • Colors of the Wind • A Dream Is a Wish Your Heart Makes • A Spoonful of Sugar • Under the Sea • A Whole New World • and more.

00416750 Book only $9.99
00416751 Book/Audio...................................$12.99

MORE EASY DUETS

arr. Carolyn Miller

9 more fun duets arranged for 1 piano, 4 hands: A Bicycle Built for Two (Daisy Bell) • Blow the Man Down • Chopsticks • Do Your Ears Hang Low? • I've Been Working on the Railroad • The Man on the Flying Trapeze • Short'nin' Bread • Skip to My Lou • The Yellow Rose of Texas.

00416832 Book only $7.99
00416833 Book/Audio...................................$10.99

MORE BROADWAY SONGS

arr. Carolyn Miller

10 more fantastic Broadway favorites arranged for a young performer, including: Castle on a Cloud • Climb Ev'ry Mountain • Gary, Indiana • In My Own Little Corner • It's the Hard-Knock Life • Memory • Oh, What a Beautiful Mornin' • Sunrise, Sunset • Think of Me • Where Is Love?

00416928 Book only $6.99
00416929 Book/Audio.................................$12.99

MORE CHILDREN'S SONGS

arr. Carolyn Miller

10 songs: The Candy Man • Do-Re-Mi • I'm Popeye the Sailor Man • It's a Small World • Linus and Lucy • The Muppet Show Theme • My Favorite Things • Sesame Street Theme • Supercalifragilisticexpialidocious • Tomorrow.

00416810 Book only $7.99
00416811 Book/Audio.................................$12.99

EXCLUSIVELY DISTRIBUTED BY

WILLIS MUSIC

HAL•LEONARD®

0820
403

FOR A COMPLETE SERIES LISTING, VISIT WWW.HALLEONARD.COM

All arrangements come with optional teacher accompaniments.